CONTENTS

2C

Mini Talk Look and listen. 03

How's the weather?

It's snowing.

Let's go outside.

Okay.

Practice

A Listen and write the letter. 🎧 05   **B** Listen and repeat. 🎧 06

| How's the weather today? | It's sunny. |

① sunny ☐   ② windy ☐   ③ cloudy ☐   ④ raining ☐   ⑤ snowing ☐

⑥ hot ☐   ⑦ cold ☐   ⑧ warm ☐   ⑨ cool ☐

Listen & Talk

A Listen and match. 07

Write & Talk

A Listen, write, and read. 🎧08

raining   weather
cloudy   have   cold

😮 How's the _____ there?

😊 It's windy and _____.

😮 Is it _____?

😊 No, it isn't.

😊 It's _____.

Do you _____ an umbrella?

😮 Yes, I do. Let's go together.

😊 Okay.

B Look and write. Then ask and answer.

How's the weather there?

cool

hot

windy

sunny

warm

snowing

1 It's _____.

2 It's _____ and _____.

3 It's _____.

4 It's _____ and _____.

Story

A Listen, write, and read.

1 How's the _____?

It's sunny.

2 Today is sunny? No! It's _____.

3 How's the weather?

It's _____.

4 Really?

Yes.

5 Oh, no! It's _____.

6 Is it _____ today?

No, it's warm.

7

8 Oh, it's _____.

cold   warm   cloudy   windy   raining   weather

B Read and check.

1

☐ It's windy.

☐ It's snowing.

2

☐ It's cloudy.

☐ It's raining.

3

☐ It's cold.

☐ It's warm.

Challenge

Draw today's weather and write.

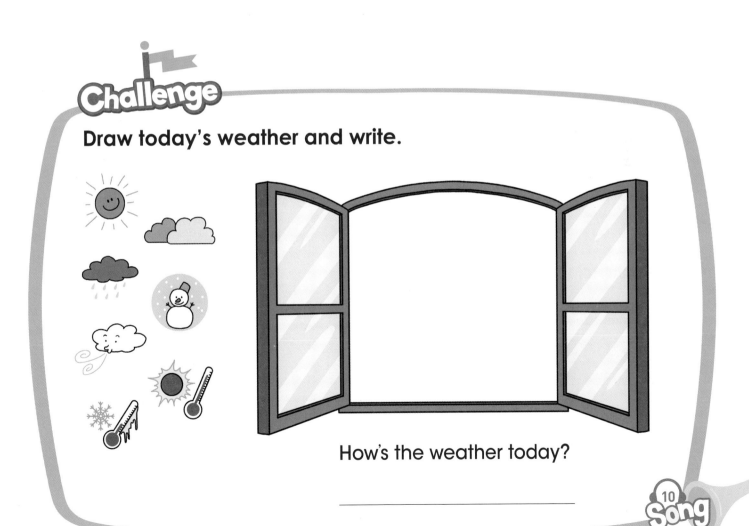

How's the weather today?

_____

Song 10

Check-Up

(A) Listen and choose. 🎧 11

1

- a
- b

2

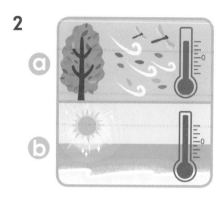
- a
- b

3

- a
- b

(B) Listen and number. 🎧 12

(C) Listen and write the letter. 🎧 13

1

_____

2

_____

3

_____

D Look and write.

1

A: How's the weather today?

B: It's _____.

2

A: How's the weather there?

B: It's _____ and _____.

3

A: It's _____.

B: Is it windy?

A: _____, it is.

E Write and say.

1 How's the weather today?

2 How's the weather there?

Put on Your Coat

Mini Talk Look and listen. ▶ 🎧16

It's cold today.
Put on your coat.

I'm not cold.

I don't like the coat.

Achoo!

Put on your coat.

Okay.

Practice

A Listen and write the letter. 🎧18

1 cold
coat ☐

2
boots ☐

hot

3
T-shirt ☐

4
shorts ☐

raining

7
raincoat ☐

B Listen and repeat. 🎧19

It's cold.
Put on your coat.

Okay.

5
hat ☐

sunny

6
sunglasses ☐

windy

8
jacket ☐

Listen & Talk

A Listen, circle, and stick. 🎧20

Write & Talk

(A) Listen, write, and read. 🎧 21

It's _____ outside.

Put on your _____.

Okay, Dad.

It's _____ now.

Take your _____.

Okay, thanks.

(B) Look and write. Then say.

shorts	jacket
pants	T-shirt

It's _____ today.

Put on your _____ and _____.

It's _____ today.

Put on your _____ and _____.

Story

Ⓐ Listen, write, and read. ▶ 🎧 22

1. It's hot.
Put on your _____.

Okay, Mom.

2. It's hot.
Put on your _____.

Okay.

3. No, Jack.
It's _____ today.

I like my _____.

4. Oh, it's _____.
Put on your sunglasses.

Okay.

5. It's cloudy.

6. It's _____!

Put on your raincoat, Jenny.

---

hot   raining   sunny   raincoat   T-shirt   shorts

B Read and match.

1

It's hot.

Put on your raincoat.

2

It's raining.

Put on your T-shirt.

3

It's sunny.

Put on your sunglasses.

Challenge

How's the weather today? Circle and write.

It's _____ today.

Put on your _____.

Song 23

Check-Up

A Listen and choose. 🎧24

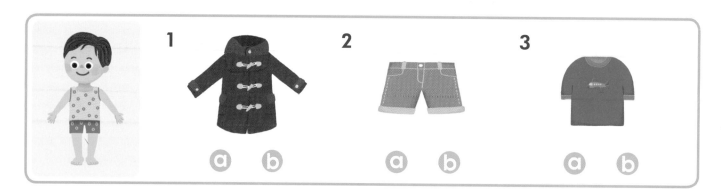

1 a b

2 a b

3 a b

B Listen, number, and match. 🎧25

C Listen and choose. 🎧26

1 a b

2 a b

3 a b

16

D Look and write.

1

A: It's cold outside.

Put on your _____.

B: Okay, Dad.

2

A: It's raining now.

Put on your _____.

B: Okay.

3

A: It's hot today.

Put on your _____.

B: Okay, Mom.

E Write and say.

1

It's windy.

_____

Okay.

2

It's sunny.

_____

Okay.

Review ①

A Complete and number.

w __ __ m ☐

__ o __ l ☐

c l __ __ d __ ☐

__ i __ __ y ☐

s __ __ w i __ __ ☐

☐ c __ __ __

☐ b __ __ __ s

☐ __ a c __ __ __

☐ T - __ __ i __ t

☐ r __ __ n c __ __ t

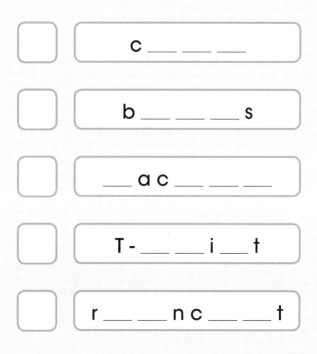

Ⓑ Read, number, and match.

1 It's windy today. Put on your jacket.	2 It's hot today. Put on your shorts.
3 It's sunny today. Put on your sunglasses.	4 It's cold today. Put on your gloves.
5 It's snowing now. Put on your hat.	6 It's raining now. Take your umbrella.

She's My Friend

Mini Talk Look and listen.  🎧29

She's strong.

Who is she?

She's my friend, Liz.

She's pretty!

🎧30 CHECK 1 a ☐ b ☐ 2 a ☐ b ☐

Practice

A Listen and write the letter. 🎧31   **B** Listen and repeat. 🎧32

mother ☐

| Who is she? | She's my mother. |
| Who is he? | He's my father. |

father ☐

brother ☐

sister ☐

me

| She's tall. | He's strong. |

tall ☐

strong ☐

old ☐

young ☐

me

Listen & Talk

A Listen and choose. 🎧33

Write & Talk

sister	cute	he
She's	He's	cool

A Listen, write, and read. 🎧 34

Look! He's _____.

Who is _____?

_____ my friend, Eric.

I have a _____.

Look. _____ my sister, Lucy.

Oh, she's very _____.

B Circle and write. Then ask and answer.

Who is she?

Who is he?

me

This is my family.

1 (He's / She's) my _____.

2 (He's / She's) my _____.

3 (He's / She's) my _____.

4 (He's / She's) my _____.

Story

Ⓐ **Listen, write, and read.** ▶ 🎧 35

She's   he   mother   father   strong   Who

B Read and match.

1

2

3

• Who is she? •

• Who is he? •

• She's my mother.

• He's my father.

• She's my sister.

Challenge

Look and write.

1 _____ my friend, Tony.

_____ _____.

2 _____ my sister, Elsa.

_____ _____.

36 Song

Check-Up

A Listen and choose. 🎧37

1

ⓐ   ⓑ

2

ⓐ   ⓑ

3

ⓐ   ⓑ

B Listen and choose. 🎧38

1

2

3

C Listen and number. 🎧39

D Write and check.

1

A: Who is _____?

B: ☐ She's my mother.

☐ He's my uncle.

2

A: Who is _____?

B: ☐ She's my sister, Amy.

☐ He's my brother, Tony.

3

A: Look! _____ my grandfather.

B: ☐ She's tall.

☐ He's strong.

E Write and say.

1

She's my mother.

2

Who is he?

Is He a Firefighter?

Mini Talk Look and listen. ▶

Who is he?
Is he a firefighter?

Yes, he is.

You're welcome.

Thank you.

He's cool.

43
CHECK 1 a ☐ b ☐ 2 a ☐ b ☐

28

Practice

A Listen and write the letter. 44   **B** Listen and repeat. 45

| Is he a pilot? | Yes, he is. | No, he isn't. |
| Is she a singer? | Yes, she is. | No, she isn't. |

1 pilot

2 singer

3 dancer

4 firefighter

5 cook

6 teacher

7 doctor

8 police officer

Listen & Talk

A Listen, number, and match. 🎧 46

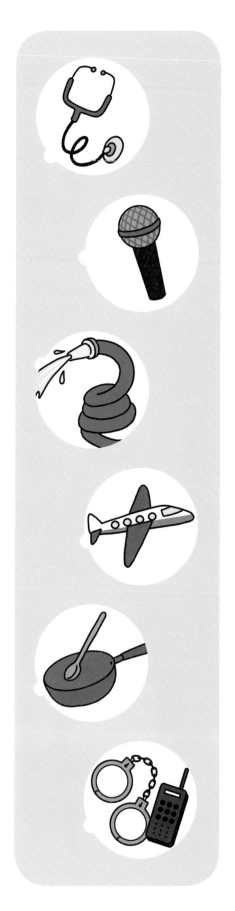

30

Write & Talk

A Listen, write, and read. 🎧47

👧 Look! He's cool!

Is he a _____?

👦 No, he isn't. He's a _____.

He's a singer, too.

👦 _____ is she?

👩 _____ my mother.

👦 Is she a _____?

👩 Yes, she is.

Yes, she/he is.

No, she/he isn't.

B Look and write. Then ask and answer.

1 Is she a firefighter?

_____, _____ _____.

2 Is he a pilot?

_____, _____ _____.

3 Is she a cook?

_____, _____ _____.

4 Is he a model?

_____, _____ _____.

Story

A Listen, write, and read.

| cook | firefighter | pilot | he | she | brother |

B Circle and match.

1  (He / She) is •   • a pilot.

2  (He / She) is •   • a cook.

3  (He / She) is •   • a firefighter.

Challenge

Look and write.

1

A: Is _____ a singer?

B: _____, _____ _____.

2

A: Is _____ a doctor?

B: _____, _____ _____.

She's a _____.

Check-Up

A Listen and circle. 🎧50

1

2

3

4

B Listen and choose. 🎧51

1

ⓐ   ⓑ

2

ⓐ   ⓑ

3

ⓐ   ⓑ

C Listen and number. 🎧52

D Look and write.

1

A: Is _____ a _____?

B: Yes, he is.

2

A: Is she a police officer?

B: _____, _____ _____.

She's a _____.

3

A: He's my dad.

B: Is _____ a doctor?

A: _____, _____ is.

E Write and say.

1

Is he a police officer?

2

Yes, she is.

Review 2

A Unscramble and number.

1 | l d o | ⋯▶ _____
2 | u y n o g | ⋯▶ _____
3 | r g t s o n | ⋯▶ _____
4 | l t l a | ⋯▶ _____

B Complete and number.

1 __ o o __   2 d __ n ____   3 __ o d __ __

4 s __ __ __ er   5 __ i __ __ t

© **Circle and write.**

1 father

2 mother

3 sister

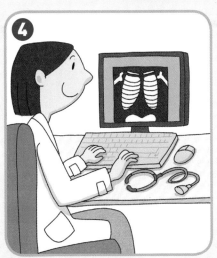
4

5

6 Weather

1 A: Who is (he / she)?

B: _____ my _____.

2 A: Who is (he / she)?

B: _____ my _____.

3 A: Who is (he / she)?

B: _____ my _____.

4 A: Is (he / she) a doctor?

B: _____

5 A: Is (he / she) a firefighter?

B: _____

6 A: Is (he / she) a teacher?

B: _____

How Old Is She?

Mini Talk Look and listen. ▶ 🎧 55

Hello.
How old are you?

I'm ten years old.

How old is she?

She's eight.

56
CHECK　1 a ☐ b ☐　2 a ☐ b ☐

Practice

Ⓐ Listen and write the letter. 🎧57

Ⓑ Listen and repeat. 🎧58

How old is he?

He's **eleven** years old.

How old is she?

She's **twelve** years old.

❶ eleven ☐

❷ twelve ☐

❸ thirteen ☐

❹ fourteen ☐

❺ fifteen ☐

❻ sixteen ☐

❼ seventeen ☐

❽ eighteen ☐

❾ nineteen ☐

Listen & Talk

A Listen and write the age. 🎧 59

Write & Talk

A Listen, write, and read. 🎧 60

| you | He's | sixteen |
| name | How old | |

🧑 This cake, please.

It's for my brother.

👩 _____ is he?

🧑 _____ nine years old.

👩 Hello. What's your _____ ?

👦 I'm Mike.

👩 How old are _____ ?

👦 I'm _____ .

B Circle and write. Then ask and answer.

| twelve | eighteen | thirteen | fourteen | fifteen |

How old is he/she?

1 (She's / He's) _____ .

2 (She's / He's) _____ .

3 (She's / He's) _____ .

4 (She's / He's) _____ .

5 (She's / He's) _____ .

Story

(A) **Listen, write, and read.** ▶ 🎧61

she   he   I'm   thirteen   twelve   How old

B Read and match.

1

2

3

She's nineteen.

She's thirteen.

She's ten.

He's twelve.

Draw your face and write.

1

Elisa, 15

She's Elisa.

_____ _____ years old.

2

My name is _____.

_____ _____ years old.

Ⓐ Listen and number. 🎧63

Ⓑ Listen and choose. 🎧64

1

Mia, 14

ⓐ   ⓑ

2

Kevin, 19

ⓐ   ⓑ

3

ⓐ   ⓑ

Ⓒ Listen and match. 🎧65

1   2   3   4

D Look and write.

1

Tina, 13

A: How old is _____?

B: She's _____.

2

Alex, 15

A: How old is _____?

B: He's _____.

3

A: You're pretty.

　　How old are _____?

B: I'm _____.

E Write and say.

1

How old is he?

2

MOVIES

She's sixteen.

What Day Is It Today?

Mini Talk Look and listen. ▶ 🎧 68

What day is it today?

FRI 7

Weekly Events
Mon.
Tue.
Wed.
Thu.
Fri.

It's Friday.

Weekly Events

Wed.	BALLOON ART	
Thu.	ROBOT MAKER	
Fri.	COOKING	

That's good!
We can cook today.

Oops!

69 CHECK　1 a ☐ b ☐　2 a ☐ b ☐

Practice

A Listen and write the letter. 70

B Listen and repeat. 71

What day is it today?

It's Sunday.

① 5 Sun. Sunday ☐

② 6 Mon. Monday ☐

③ 7 Tue. Tuesday ☐

④ 8 Wed. Wednesday ☐

⑤ 9 Thu. Thursday ☐

⑥ 10 Fri. Friday ☐

⑦ 11 Sat. Saturday ☐

Listen & Talk

A Listen and stick. 72

1

Sticker

2

Sticker

3

Sticker

4

Sticker

5

Sticker

6

Sticker

7

Sticker

8

Sticker

Write & Talk

Ⓐ Listen, write, and read. 🎧 73

it	like	have
Tuesday		Thursday

👦 It's _____ today.

We _____ fish and salad.

👦 Do you _____ fish?

👦 No, I don't.

👧 What day is _____ today?

👧 It's _____.

Today is my birthday.

👧 That's great. Happy birthday!

Ⓑ Look and write. Then ask and answer.

What day is it today?

1 Today is _____.

2 Today is _____.

3 Today is _____.

4 Today is _____.

Story

Ⓐ **Listen, write, and read.** ▶ 🎧 74

today   Saturday   Friday   Wednesday   What day   swim

50

B Read and match.

1  • • It's Saturday. • • I can cook.

2  • • It's Thursday. • • I can play.

3  • • It's Wednesday. • • I can swim.

Challenge

Complete and write.

S_____

M_____

T_____

W_____

T_____

F_____

S_____

_____ _____ is it today?

_____ _____.

Check-Up

Ⓐ Listen and choose. 🎧76

1
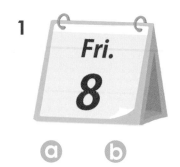
Fri.
8

ⓐ　ⓑ

2
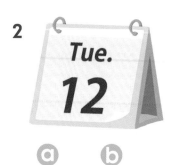
Tue.
12

ⓐ　ⓑ

3

Wed.
7

ⓐ　ⓑ

Ⓑ Listen and number. 🎧77

Saturday ☐　　　Tuesday ☐　　　Sunday ☐

Ⓒ Listen and match. 🎧78

1 　**2** 　**3** 　**4**

Monday　　　Friday　　　Wednesday　　　Thursday

D Look and write.

1
? Thu.

A: What day is _____ today?

B: _____ _____.

2
Sports Center
Fri.   Sat.   Sun.

A: _____ _____ is it today?

B: _____ _____.

We can ski today.

3
MENU
Thu.   Fri.

A: What day is it _____?

B: _____ _____.

We have pizza today.

E Write and say.

1
What day is it today?

8
TUE   WED   THU
      5   6

2
What day is it today?

Tue.
15

A **Choose and write.**

nineteen	eleven	sixteen	fourteen	eighteen
twelve	Wednesday	Monday	Saturday	Thursday

1 _____ ➡ 2 _____ ➡ thirteen

3 _____ ➡ fifteen ➡ 4 _____

seventeen ➡ 5 _____ ➡ 6 _____

Sunday ➡ 7 _____ ➡ Tuesday

8 _____ ➡ 9 _____ ➡ Friday

10 _____

Ⓑ Look and write.

1 A: How old is _____?

   B: _____ _____.

2 A: How old is _____?

   B: _____ _____.

3 A: How old is _____?

   B: _____ _____.

4 A: How old is _____?

   B: _____ _____.

Ⓒ Look and write.

1 A: What day is it today?

   B: It's _____.

2 A: What day is it today?

   B: It's _____.

3 A: It's _____.

   B: I can skate today.

4 A: It's _____.

   B: I can cook today.

It Has Big Wings

Mini Talk Look and listen.

82
CHECK 1 a ☐ b ☐ 2 a ☐ b ☐

56

Practice

A Listen and write the letter. 🎧 83   **B** Listen and repeat. 🎧 84

Look at the giraffe. | It has a long neck.

giraffe

1 a long neck ☐

2 long legs ☐

3 big ears ☐

elephant

4 a long nose ☐

5 big feet ☐

6 small eyes ☐

9 small wings ☐

7 a big mouth ☐

8 a short tail ☐

bird

hippo

Listen & Talk

Listen and circle. 🎧85

Write & Talk

A Listen, write, and read. 🎧 86

Is this a _____?

Yes, it is.

It has big _____.

It has a _____ tail, too.

Look at the _____!

It's _____.

It has a long _____.

I like giraffes.

B Circle and write. Then say.

tail   legs   ears   eyes

1   It has (long / short) _____.

2   It has (big / small) _____.

3   It has (big / small) _____.

4   It has a (long / short) _____.

Story

(A) Listen, write, and read. ▶ 🎧 87

1 It has long ears.
It has a _____ tail.
What is it?

2 Is it a _____?

Yes, it is.

3 It has a big _____.
It's gray. What is it?

4 Is it a _____?

Yes, that's right!

5 It's small.
It has a _____ tail.

6 Is it a _____?

Yes, that's right!

7 Ahhh!

long   short   nose   koala   mouse   rabbit

B Look and circle.

1

It has long (ears / legs).

2

It has a big (mouth / nose).

3

It has a (long / short) tail.

Check and write.

Look at the _____.

It has _____ _____.

Check-Up

A Listen and choose. 🎧89

1
ⓐ ⓑ

2
ⓐ ⓑ

3
ⓐ ⓑ

B Listen and mark ○ or ✕. 🎧90

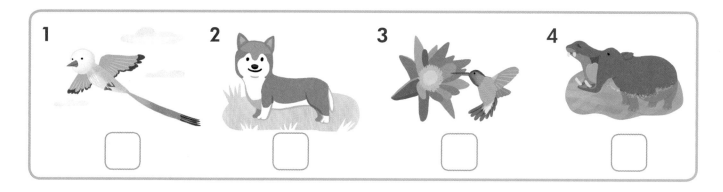

1 ⬜ 2 ⬜ 3 ⬜ 4 ⬜

C Listen and choose. 🎧91

1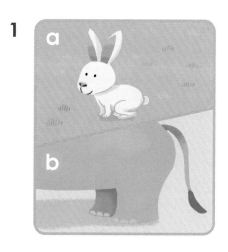

2

3

D Circle and write.

1

A: Look at the dog.

B: It has (big / small) _____.

2

A: Look! It's a monkey.

B: It has a (long / short) _____.

It's cute.

3

A: It has (long / short) _____.

B: Is it a pig?

A: Yes, it is.

E Write and say.

1

Look at the bird.

2

Look at the hippo.

I'm in the Bathroom

Mini Talk Look and listen. ▶ 🎧94

Where are you, Sam?

I'm here.
I'm in the bathroom.

Where is Jack?

He's in the bathroom, too.

🎧95 CHECK 1 a ☐ b ☐ 2 a ☐ b ☐

Practice

A Listen and write the letter. 🎧96 **B** Listen and repeat. 🎧97

Where is she?
She's in the living room.

Where is he?
He's in the bathroom.

1 living room ☐

2 bedroom ☐

3 bathroom ☐

4 kitchen ☐

5 dining room ☐

6 yard ☐

me

Listen & Talk

A Listen and match. 🎧 98

1    **2**    **3**

4    **5**    **6**    **7**

Write & Talk

A Listen, write, and read. 🎧99

you	in	Where
living room		kitchen

Mom, I'm home.

Hi, Tina.

_____ is Dad?

He's in the _____.

Where are _____, Billy?

I'm in the _____.

Where is Bella?

She's _____ the yard.

B Look and write. Then ask and answer.

bathroom   bedroom   living room   dining room

Where are you?

1 I'm in the _____.

2 I'm in the _____.

3 I'm _____.

4 I'm _____.

Story

Ⓐ Listen, write, and read. ▶ 🎧100

1 Where are you, Jack?

I'm in the _____.

2 Where is Kate?

She's in the _____.

3 That's good.

4 Where is Mom?

She's in the _____.

5 Jack! Kate! _____ are you?

6 Where is Jack?

He's in the _____.

7 Jack! Kate!

| Where | yard | bedroom | kitchen | living room |

B Read and circle.

1  He's in the (living room / dining room).

2  She's in the (bathroom / bedroom).

3  She's in the (yard / kitchen).

Stick, circle, and write.

1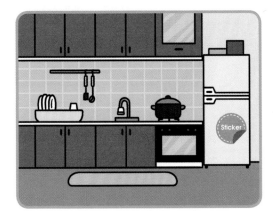

Where is (he / she)?

_____ in the _____.

2

Where is (he / she)?

_____ in the _____.

Check-Up

A Listen and choose. 🎧102

1

ⓐ ⓑ

2
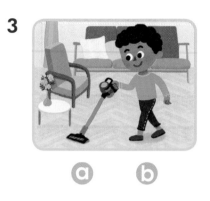
ⓐ ⓑ

3

ⓐ ⓑ

B Listen and number. 🎧103

C Listen and mark ○ or ✕. 🎧104

1

2

3

70

D Circle and write.

1

A: Where is Mom?

B: (He's / She's) in the _____.

2

A: Where is Grandpa?

B: (He's / She's) in the _____.

3

A: Where are you, Ben?

B: (I'm / They're) in the _____.

E Write and say.

1 Where is Dad?

2 Where is Ann?

A Look and write.

a mouth	a neck	a nose	feet	eyes
kitchen	yard	dining room	bedroom	

1

_____

2

_____

3

_____

4

_____

5

_____

6

_____

7

_____

8

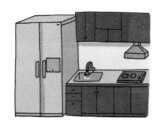

_____

9

_____

B **Number and match.**

☐ Look at the bird. •   • It has big ears.

☐ Look at the hippo. •   • It has a long tail.

☐ Look at the elephant. •   • It has small wings.

☐ Look at the monkey. •   • It has short legs.

C **Circle and write.**

kitchen   bathroom   bedroom   living room

1 A: Where is (she / he)?

   B: _____ in the _____.

2 A: Where is (she / he)?

   B: _____ in the _____.

3 A: Where is (she / he)?

   B: _____ in the _____.

4 A: Where is (she / he)?

   B: _____ in the _____.

Songs

Unit 1 How's the Weather? 🎧10

How's the weather?

It's sunny.

It's windy. It's cool!

How's the weather?

It's raining.

It's snowing. It's cold!

Unit 2 Put On Your Coat 🎧23

It's cold.

Put on your coat. Put on your boots.

Okay.

It's hot.

Put on your shorts. Put on your T-shirt.

Okay.

Unit 3 Who Is She? 🎧36

Who is she? Who is she?

She's my mother. She's tall.

She's my sister. She's pretty.

Who is he? Who is he?

He's my father. He's strong.

He's my brother. He's cute.

Unit 4 Is He a Singer? 🎧49

Look! Is he a singer?

Yes, he is. He's a singer.

Look! Is she a cook?

Yes, she is. She's a cook.

Is he a police officer?

No, he isn't. He's a pilot.

Oh, he's cool!

Unit 5   How Old Is She? 🎧62

This is my sister.

   How old is she?

She's ten years old.

This is my friend.

   How old is he?

He's eleven years old.

Unit 6   What Day Is It Today? 🎧75

Sunday, Monday,

Tuesday, Wednesday,

Thursday, Friday, Saturday!

What day is it today?

   It's Monday. It's chicken day!

What day is it today?

   It's Friday. It's pizza day. Yeah!

Unit 7   It Has Small Wings 🎧88

Look! It's a bird.

It has small wings.

   Look! It's an elephant.

   It has a long nose.

Look! It's a hippo.

It has a big mouth.

It has a short tail, too.

Unit 8   Where Are You, Kevin? 🎧101

Where is Mom?

   In the bedroom.

   She's in the bedroom.

Where is Dad?

   In the kitchen.

   He's in the kitchen.

Where are you, Kevin?

   I'm here.

   I'm in the bathroom.

A Listen and repeat. Then read. 105

-ch
-sh
-th

1 ch → bench
2 ch → lunch

3 sh → fish
4 sh → wash

5 th → math
6 th → bath

B Listen and check. 106

1 ☐ ch ☐ sh ☐ th
2 ☐ ch ☐ sh ☐ th

3 ☐ ch ☐ sh ☐ th
4 ☐ ch ☐ sh ☐ th

C Match and write.

1 • • ma • • sh → ☐

2  • • ben • • ch → ☐

3  • • fi • • th → ☐

Phonics ②

(A) Listen and repeat. Then read. 🎧107

1 **ng** → sing

2 **ng** → wing

3 **ng** → long

4 **nk** → pink

5 **nk** → bank

6 **nk** → drink

(B) Listen and check. 🎧108

1
☐ wing
☐ bank

2
☐ sing
☐ pink

3
☐ long
☐ drink

4
☐ wing
☐ pink

(C) Match and write.

1  wi •
 • ng
 • nk

_____

2 pi •
• ng
• nk

_____

3  dri •
• ng
• nk

_____

4 lo •
• ng
• nk

_____

A Listen and repeat. Then read. 🎧109

cl
gl
pl

1 cl → clock

2 cl → class

3 gl → glass

4 gl → glove

5 pl → plane

6 pl → plate

B Listen and circle. 🎧110

1
clock
glass

2
class
plate

3
glove
plane

4
clock
class

C Match and write.

1  • • pl • • ock [   ]

2  • • cl • • ass [   ]

3 • • gl • • ane  [   ]

Ⓐ Listen and repeat. Then read. 🎧111

bl **fl** **sl**	1 **bl** → black	2 **bl** → block
	3 **fl** → flag	4 **fl** → flute
	5 **sl** → sled	6 **sl** → slide

Ⓑ Listen and match. 🎧112

1 fl •   • ag
   bl •   • ack

2 sl •   • ag
   fl •   • ed

3 sl •   • ute
   fl •   • ide

4 bl •   • ide
   sl •   • ock

Ⓒ Circle and write.

1   bl
     fl

_____ute

2   fl
     sl

_____ed

3   bl
     sl

_____ack

Ⓐ Listen and repeat. Then read. 🎧113

br cr dr	1	br → brush	2	br → brown
	3	cr → crab	4	cr → crown
	5	dr → dress	6	dr → drive

Ⓑ Listen and check. 🎧114

1 ☐ brown ☐ drive   2 ☐ crown ☐ dress

3 ☐ dress ☐ brush   4 ☐ crab ☐ drive

Ⓒ Circle and write.

1

br   cr

_____ab

2

dr   br

_____ush

3

dr   cr

_____ess

80

Phonics 6

(A) Listen and repeat. Then read. 🎧115

fr	1 fr → frog	2 fr → frame
gr	3 gr → grass	4 gr → green
tr	5 tr → truck	6 tr → tree

(B) Listen and circle. 🎧116

1 tree / frog

2 frame / grass

3 green / truck

4 frame / grass

(C) Match and write.

1 • • tr • • uck ➡ ☐

2 • • fr • • een ➡ ☐

3 • • gr • • og ➡ ☐

A Listen, circle, and write. 🎧117

1 fl pl cl —— _____ ane

2 gl bl sl —— _____ ove

3 tr gr fr —— _____ uck

4 br cr dr —— _____ ive

B Listen, circle, and match. 🎧118

1 glass
   class

2 green
   frame

3 sled
   flag

4 block
   brush

•   •   •   •

C Circle and write.

1 tr   cr

_____ ab

2

bl   gl

_____ ack

3

fr   dr

_____ og

Ⓐ Listen and repeat. Then read. 119

y

1 y → happy

2 y → sunny

3 y → windy

4 y → fly

5 y → cry

6 y → sky

Ⓑ Listen and check. 120

1 ☐ sunny ☐ sky

2 ☐ sunny ☐ fly

3 ☐ happy ☐ cry

4 ☐ windy ☐ fly

Ⓒ Look and write.

1  _____y

2  _____y

3  _____y

Word List 2C

Unit 1 How's the Weather?

cloudy _____

cold _____

cool _____

hot _____

raining _____

snowing _____

sunny _____

today _____

warm _____

weather _____

windy _____

Unit 2 Put On Your Coat

boots _____

coat _____

gloves _____

hat _____

jacket _____

now _____

put on _____

raincoat _____

shorts _____

sunglasses _____

take _____

T-shirt _____

Unit 3 She's My Friend

cool _____

cute _____

he _____

old _____

pretty _____

strong _____

she _____

tall _____

who _____

young _____

Unit 4 Is He a Firefighter?

cook _____

dance _____

dancer _____

doctor _____

firefighter _____

model _____

pilot _____

police officer _____

singer _____

teacher _____

Unit 5 How Old Is She?

eight _____

eighteen _____

eleven _____

fifteen _____

fourteen _____

nine _____

nineteen _____

seventeen _____

sixteen _____

ten _____

thirteen _____

twelve _____

Unit 6 What Day Is It Today?

birthday _____

day _____

Friday _____

Monday _____

Saturday _____

Sunday _____

Thursday _____

today _____

Tuesday _____

Wednesday _____

Unit 7 It Has Big Wings

a mouth _____

a neck _____

a nose _____

a tail _____

big _____

ears _____

eyes _____

feet _____

legs _____

long _____

short _____

small _____

wings _____

Unit 8 I'm in the Bathroom

bathroom _____

bedroom _____

dining room _____

here _____

in _____

kitchen _____

living room _____

where _____

yard _____

Syllabus 2C

Unit 1 How's the Weather?

Structures	Vocabulary		Phonics
• How's the weather (there)?	sunny	hot	Consonant Digraphs
It's snowing.	windy	cold	Ending -ch, -sh, -th
• It's windy and cloudy.	cloudy	warm	
• Is it cold? Yes, it is. / No, it isn't.	raining	cool	
• Let's go outside. Okay.	snowing	weather	

Unit 2 Put on Your Coat

Structures	Vocabulary		Phonics
• It's cold. Put on your coat.	coat	jacket	Consonant Digraphs
Okay.	boots	put on	Ending –ng, -nk
• Put on your T-shirt and shorts.	shorts	cold	
• I'm not cold.	T-shirt	hot	
• It's raining now.	hat	sunny	
• Take your umbrella.	sunglasses	raining	
	raincoat	windy	
Review 1			

Unit 3 She's My Friend

Structures	Vocabulary		Phonics
• Who is she/he?	tall	mother	Consonant Digraphs
She's my mother. / He's my father.	strong	father	cl, gl, pl
• She's/He's (very) tall.	old	sister	
• I have a brother.	young	brother	
	cute	grandfather	
	pretty	grandmother	
	cool		

Unit 4 Is He a Firefighter?

Structures	Vocabulary		Phonics
• Is he/she a singer?	singer	teacher	Consonant Digraphs
Yes, he/she is. / No, he/she isn't.	dancer	firefighter	bl, fl, sl
• He's/She's a firefighter.	doctor	police officer	
• Who is she? She's my mother.	cook	model	
	pilot		
Review 2			

Unit 5 How Old Is She?

Structures	Vocabulary		Phonics

• How old is she/he?
  She's/He's eleven (years old).
• How old are you?
  I'm ten (years old).
• Is he your brother? Yes, he is. / No, he isn't.
	eleven
	twelve
	thirteen
	fourteen
	fifteen
		sixteen
		seventeen
		eighteen
		nineteen
			Consonant Digraphs
			br, cr, dr

Unit 6 What Day Is It Today?

Structures	Vocabulary		Phonics
• What day is it today? It's Sunday. • We can cook today. • We have fish and salad. • Today is my birthday. • Do you like fish? Yes, I do. / No, I don't.	Sunday Monday Tuesday Wednesday Thursday	Friday Saturday day today birthday	Consonant Digraphs fr, gr, tr
Review 3			

Unit 7 It Has Big Wings

Structures	Vocabulary		Phonics
• Look at the giraffe. It has long legs. • It's tall. • Is it a kangaroo? Yes, it is. • I like giraffes.	a neck a nose a mouth a tail ears eyes legs	wings feet big small long short	Review: Consonant Digraphs

Unit 8 I'm in the Bathroom

Structures	Vocabulary		Phonics

• Where is he/she?
  He's/She's in the living room.
• Where are you?
  I'm in the bathroom.
• I'm here. I'm in the bathroom.
	living room
	bedroom
	bathroom
	dining room
		kitchen
		yard
		where
		in
			Vowel y

Review 4			

11 Read and choose.
다음을 읽고 알맞은 그림을 고르세요.

He's a firefighter.

ⓐ

ⓑ

ⓒ

ⓓ

[12-13] Look and choose.
그림을 보고 알맞은 것을 고르세요.

12

ⓐ Put on your raincoat. – Okay.
ⓑ Put on your shorts. – Okay.
ⓒ Put on your boots. – Okay.
ⓓ Put on your jacket. – Okay.

13

ⓐ Who is she? – She's my mother.
ⓑ Who is she? – She's my grandmother.
ⓒ Who is he? – He's my brother.
ⓓ Who is he? – He's my grandfather.

14 Unscramble and write.
단어를 배열하여 문장을 완성하세요.

(she / Is / a model / ?)

_____

15 Look and write.
그림을 보고 빈칸에 알맞은 말을 쓰세요.

It's _____ .

16 Read and match.
알맞은 문장이 되도록 선으로 연결하세요.

ⓐ Is he • • your hat.

ⓑ Put on • • a singer?

[17-18] Read and choose.
대화의 빈칸에 알맞은 것을 고르세요.

17

A: Is she a police officer?
B: _____ She's a cook.

ⓐ Yes, he is.
ⓑ Yes, she is.
ⓒ No, he isn't.
ⓓ No, she isn't.

18

A: Who is he?
B: _____

ⓐ She's strong.
ⓑ He's tall.
ⓒ He's my father.
ⓓ She's my sister.

[19-20] Look and write.
그림을 보고 대화를 완성하세요.

19

A: _____ hot today.
B: Okay.

_____ on your _____ .

20

A: Look! He's my _____ .
B: He's _____ .

Midterm TEST 2C

Institute	
Name	
Score	/100

[1-2] Listen and choose.
잘 듣고 알맞은 그림을 고르세요.

1

ⓐ 　ⓑ

ⓒ 　ⓓ

2

ⓐ 　ⓑ

ⓒ 　ⓓ

3 Listen and choose.
잘 듣고 그림에 알맞은 것을 고르세요.

ⓐ　ⓑ　ⓒ　ⓓ

[4-5] Listen and mark O or X.
잘 듣고 그림과 일치하면 ○표, 일치하지 않으면 X 표를 하세요.

4

(　)

5

(　)

[6-7] Listen and choose.
잘 듣고 그림에 알맞은 대화를 고르세요.

6

ⓐ　ⓑ　ⓒ　ⓓ

7

ⓐ　ⓑ　ⓒ　ⓓ

8 Listen and choose.
잘 듣고 알맞은 그림을 고르세요.

ⓐ 　ⓑ

ⓒ 　ⓓ

[9-10] Listen and choose.
잘 듣고 알맞은 응답을 고르세요.

9　ⓐ Yes, I am.　ⓑ No, I'm not.
　　ⓒ Yes, it is.　ⓓ No, I don't.

10　ⓐ He's cute.　ⓑ He's my brother.
　　ⓒ She's old.　ⓓ She's my sister.

11

It has big eyes.

ⓐ

ⓑ

ⓒ

ⓓ

[12-13] Look and choose.
그림을 보고 알맞은 것을 고르세요.

12

ⓐ He's in the kitchen.

ⓑ She's in the bedroom.

ⓒ He's in the living room.

ⓓ She's in the bathroom.

13

ⓐ How old is she? – She's ten.

ⓑ How old is he? – He's twelve.

ⓒ How old are you? – I'm sixteen.

ⓓ How old is he? – He's eleven.

14 Look and write.
그림을 보고 빈칸에 알맞은 말을 쓰세요.

It's _____ .

15 Unscramble and write.
단어를 배열하여 문장을 쓰세요.

(has / legs / It / short / .)

_____

16 Read and match.
알맞은 문장이 되도록 선을 연결하세요.

ⓐ It's •   • is she?

ⓑ She's •   • Tuesday.

ⓒ How old •   • in the yard.

[17-18] Read and choose.
대화의 빈칸에 알맞은 것을 고르세요.

17

A: Where is Kevin?

B: _____

ⓐ I'm nineteen.

ⓑ He's in the bedroom.

ⓒ I'm in the dining room.

ⓓ She's thirteen years old.

18

A: _____

B: It's Sunday.

ⓐ How old is she?

ⓑ Where are you?

ⓒ How's the weather today?

ⓓ What day is it today?

[19-20] Look and write.
그림을 보고 대화를 완성하세요.

19

A: Look at the _____ .

B: It has a _____ .

20

A: How old is _____ ?

B: She's _____ years old.

Final TEST 2c

Institute ____

Name ____

Score ____ /100

[1-2] Listen and choose.
잘 듣고 알맞은 그림을 고르세요.

1
ⓐ  11
ⓑ 12
ⓒ 17
ⓓ 18

2
ⓐ
ⓑ
ⓒ
ⓓ

3 Listen and choose.
잘 듣고 그림에 알맞은 말을 고르세요.

ⓐ ⓑ ⓒ ⓓ

[4-5] Listen and mark O or X.
잘 듣고 그림과 일치하면 O표, 일치하지 않으면 X표를 하세요.

4

( )

5

( )

[6-7] Listen and choose.
잘 듣고 그림에 알맞은 대화를 고르세요.

6

ⓐ ⓑ ⓒ ⓓ

7

ⓐ ⓑ ⓒ ⓓ

8 Listen and choose.
잘 듣고 알맞은 그림을 고르세요.

ⓐ  Thu.
ⓑ  Thu.
ⓒ Wed.
ⓓ Wed.

[9-10] Listen and choose.
잘 듣고 알맞은 응답을 고르세요.

9
ⓐ She's in the bathroom.
ⓑ He's in the bedroom.
ⓒ I'm in the dining room.
ⓓ He's in the yard, too.

10
ⓐ She's eleven.　　ⓑ He's fifteen.
ⓒ I'm sixteen.　　ⓓ He's Jack.

Let's Go · 2C

Unit **2** p. 12

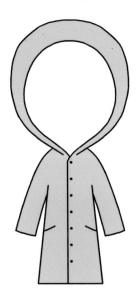

Unit **6** p. 48

Friday	Tuesday	Saturday	Wednesday
Thursday	Sunday	Tuesday	Monday

Unit **8** p. 69

2nd Edition

LET'S GO

2c

to the English World

Word Book
& Workbook

CHUNJAE EDUCATION, INC.

Word Book

UNIT 1 How's the Weather?

Ⓐ Listen and repeat.

sunny
화창한

It's sunny.
화창해.

windy
바람 부는

It's windy.
바람이 불어.

cloudy
흐린, 구름 낀

It's cloudy.
흐려.

raining
비 오는

It's raining.
비가 와.

snowing
눈 오는

It's snowing.
눈이 와.

hot
더운

It's hot.
더워.

cold
추운

It's cold.
추워.

warm
따뜻한

It's warm.
따뜻해.

cool
시원한

It's cool.
시원해.

1 **sunny**
화창한

2 **windy**
바람 부는

3 **cloudy**
흐린, 구름 낀

4 **raining**
비 오는

5 **snowing**
눈 오는

6 **hot**
더운

7 **cold**
추운

8 **warm**
따뜻한

9 **cool**
시원한

Learn More

today 오늘	It's cold today. 오늘은 추워.
weather 날씨	How's the weather? 날씨가 어때?
Let's go outside. 밖으로 나가자.	

UNIT 2 Put on Your Coat

A **Listen and repeat.**

coat
코트

Put on your coat.
코트를 입어.

boots
부츠

Put on your boots.
부츠를 신어.

T-shirt
티셔츠

Put on your T-shirt.
티셔츠를 입어.

shorts
반바지

Put on your shorts.
반바지를 입어.

hat
모자

Put on your hat.
모자를 써.

sunglasses
선글라스

Put on your sunglasses.
선글라스를 껴.

raincoat
비옷

Put on your raincoat.
비옷을 입어.

jacket
재킷

Put on your jacket.
재킷을 입어.

put on
~을 입다

Put on your coat.
코트를 입어.

B Read, write, and say.

□Read □Write □Say

1 **coat**
코트

2 **boots**
부츠

3 **T-shirt**
티셔츠

4 **shorts**
반바지

5 **hat**
모자

6 **sunglasses**
선글라스

7 **raincoat**
비옷

8 **jacket**
재킷

9 **put on**
~을 입다

Learn More

outside 밖에

now 지금

take 가져가다

gloves (손가락 모양의) 장갑

It's cold outside. 밖은 추워.

It's raining now. 지금 비가 와.

Take your umbrella. 우산을 가져가.

UNIT 3 She's My Friend

A Listen and repeat.

pretty
예쁜

She's pretty.
그녀는 예뻐.

tall
키가 큰

He's tall.
그는 키가 커.

strong
힘이 센

She's strong.
그녀는 힘이 세.

old
나이가 많은

He's old.
그는 나이가 많으셔.

young
어린

She's young.
그녀는 어려.

cute
귀여운

He's cute.
그는 귀여워.

cool
멋진

She's cool.
그녀는 멋져.

6

B Read, write, and say.

1 pretty
에쁜

2 tall
키가 큰

3 strong
힘이 센

4 old
나이가 많은

5 young
어린

6 cute
귀여운

7 cool
멋진

Learn More

she 그녀	mother 어머니	grandmother 할머니
he 그	father 아버지	grandfather 할아버지
who 누구	brother 형, 오빠, 남동생	uncle 삼촌, 숙부
	sister 누나, 언니, 여동생	aunt 이모, 고모, 숙모

UNIT 4 Is He a Firefighter?

 Listen and repeat.

pilot
파일럿, 조종사

He's a pilot.
그는 파일럿이야.

singer
가수

She's a singer.
그녀는 가수야.

dancer
댄서

He's a dancer.
그는 댄서야.

firefighter
소방관

She's a firefighter.
그녀는 소방관이야.

cook
요리사

He's a cook.
그는 요리사야.

teacher
선생님

Is she a teacher?
그녀는 선생님이니?

doctor
의사

Is he a doctor?
그는 의사니?

police officer
경찰관

Is she a police officer?
그녀는 경찰관이니?

model
모델

Is he a model?
그는 모델이니?

B Read, write, and say.

Read ☐ Write ☐ Say ☐

1 pilot
파일럿, 조종사

2 singer
가수

3 dancer
댄서

4 firefighter
소방관

5 cook
요리사

6 teacher
선생님

7 doctor
의사

8 police officer
경찰관

9 model
모델

Learn More

Are you a cook? 당신은 요리사인가요?

Yes, I am. / No, I'm not. 응, 그래요. / 아니, 그렇지 않아요.

Unit 4 **9**

How Old Is She?

A Listen and repeat. 53 54

11	eleven 11, 열하나	I'm eleven. 나는 열한 살이야.
12	twelve 12, 열둘	I'm twelve. 나는 열두 살이야.
13	thirteen 13, 열셋	I'm thirteen. 나는 열세 살이야.
14	fourteen 14, 열넷	She's fourteen. 그녀는 열네 살이야.
15	fifteen 15, 열다섯	He's fifteen. 그는 열다섯 살이야.
16	sixteen 16, 열여섯	She's sixteen. 그녀는 열여섯 살이야.
17	seventeen 17, 열일곱	He's seventeen. 그는 열일곱 살이야.
18	eighteen 18, 열여덟	She's eighteen. 그녀는 열여덟 살이야.
19	nineteen 19, 열아홉	He's nineteen. 그는 열아홉 살이야.

B Read, write, and say.

☐ Read ☐ Write ☐ Say

1 eleven
11, 열하나

2 twelve
12, 열둘

3 thirteen
13, 열셋

4 fourteen
14, 열넷

5 fifteen
15, 열다섯

6 sixteen
16, 열여섯

7 seventeen
17, 열일곱

8 eighteen
18, 열여덟

9 nineteen
19, 열아홉

Learn More

How old are you? 너는 몇 살이니?

How old is he? 그는 몇 살이니?

How old is she? 그녀는 몇 살이니?

〈Numbers 1-10〉

one   two   three   four   five

six   seven   eight   nine   ten

Unit 5   **11**

UNIT 6 — What Day Is It Today?

A Listen and repeat.

Sun.	**Sunday** 일요일	**It's Sunday.** 일요일이야.
Mon.	**Monday** 월요일	**It's Monday.** 월요일이야.
Tue.	**Tuesday** 화요일	**It's Tuesday.** 화요일이야.
Wed.	**Wednesday** 수요일	**It's Wednesday.** 수요일이야.
Thu.	**Thursday** 목요일	**It's Thursday.** 목요일이야.
Fri.	**Friday** 금요일	**It's Friday.** 금요일이야.
Sat.	**Saturday** 토요일	**It's Saturday.** 토요일이야.

today
오늘

What day is it today?
오늘이 무슨 요일이야?

☐ Read ☐ Write ☐ Say

1 Sunday
일요일

2 Monday
월요일

3 Tuesday
화요일

4 Wednesday
수요일

5 Thursday
목요일

6 Friday
금요일

7 Saturday
토요일

8 today
오늘

Learn More

what day 무슨 요일	What day is it today? 오늘이 무슨 요일이야?
birthday 생일	Today is my birthday. 오늘은 내 생일이야.
cook 요리하다	We can cook today. 우리는 오늘 요리할 수 있어.

UNIT 7 It Has Big Wings

Ⓐ Listen and repeat. 79 80

	a neck 목	It has a long neck. 그것은 긴 목을 가지고 있어.
	legs 다리 (a leg 한쪽 다리)	It has long legs. 그것은 긴 다리를 가지고 있어.
	ears 귀 (an ear 한쪽 귀)	It has big ears. 그것은 큰 귀를 가지고 있어.
	a nose 코	It has a long nose. 그것은 긴 코를 가지고 있어.
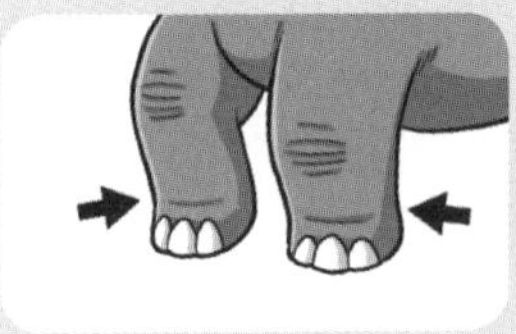	feet 발 (a foot 한쪽 발)	It has big feet. 그것은 큰 발을 가지고 있어.
	eyes 눈 (an eye 한쪽 눈)	It has small eyes. 그것은 작은 눈을 가지고 있어.
	a mouth 입	It has a big mouth. 그것은 큰 입을 가지고 있어.
	a tail 꼬리	It has a tail. 그것은 꼬리가 있어.
	wings 날개 (a wing 한쪽 날개)	It has wings. 그것은 날개가 있어.

1 **a neck**
목

2 **legs**
다리

3 **ears**
귀

4 **a nose**
코

5 **feet**
발

6 **eyes**
눈

7 **a mouth**
입

8 **a tail**
꼬리

9 **wings**
날개

Learn More

big (크기가) 큰 ⟷ **small** (크기가) 작은   **long** (길이가) 긴 ⟷ **short** (길이가) 짧은

I'm in the Bathroom

A Listen and repeat.

living room
거실

I'm in the living room.
나는 거실에 있어.

bedroom
침실

I'm in the bedroom.
나는 침실에 있어.

bathroom
욕실

I'm in the bathroom.
나는 욕실에 있어.

kitchen
부엌

He's in the kitchen.
그는 부엌에 있어.

dining room
식당 (식탁이 놓인 방)

She's in the dining room.
그녀는 식당에 있어.

yard
마당

He's in the yard.
그는 마당에 있어.

in
~ 안에

It's in the box.
그것은 상자 안에 있어.

where
어디에

Where are you, Sam?
너 어디에 있니, 샘?

B **Read, write, and say.**

☐Read ☐Write ☐Say

1 **living room**
거실

2 **bedroom**
침실

3 **bathroom**
욕실

4 **kitchen**
부엌

5 **dining room**
식당

6 **yard**
마당

7 **in**
~안에

8 **where**
어디에

Learn More

I'm here. 나 여기에 있어.

Mom, I'm home. 엄마, 저 집에 왔어요.

Workbook

How's the Weather?

Words

(A) Match and write.

1
_____

warm •

cloudy •

6
_____

2
_____

snowing •

cold •

7
_____

3
_____

sunny •

cool •

8
_____

4
_____

windy •

hot •

5
_____

raining •

9
_____

Practice

(A) Read and check.

1 It's raining.

☐   ☐

2 It's cloudy.

☐   ☐

3 It's hot.

☐   ☐

4 It's sunny.

☐   ☐

(B) Circle and write.

1

A: How's the weather?

B: It's _____.
   (windy / snowing)

2

A: How's the weather today?

B: It's _____.
   (cool / cold)

Listen & Talk

Ⓐ Match and trace.

1    How's the weather? •   • It's raining.

2    How's the weather? •   • It's sunny.

3    How's the weather? •   • It's windy.

4    How's the weather? •   • It's snowing.

Ⓑ Look and write.

| warm | cloudy | sunny | windy |

1

A: How's the weather today?

B: It's _____ and _____.

2

A: How's the weather there?

B: It's _____ and _____.

Write & Talk

(A) Look and write.

1

A: How's the weather?

B: It's _____ .

2

A: How's the _____ today?

B: It's _____ and cold.

3

A: It's _____ .

B: Is it hot?

A: _____ , it is.

4

A: _____ the weather there?

B: It's windy and _____ .

A: Is _____ cold?

B: No, _____ _____ .

5

A: It's _____ .

I _____ have an _____ .

B: I have an umbrella. Let's go together.

Story

Ⓐ Look and write.

| No, it's warm. | Oh, no! It's raining | It's cloudy. |

1 How's the weather?

2 Is it cold today?

Ⓑ Look and write.

1

A: How's the weather there?

B: It's _____.

A: Is it hot?

B: _____, _____ _____.

2

A: How's the weather there?

B: It's _____.

A: Is it cold?

B: _____, _____ _____.

Writing

Ⓐ Make the sentence.

1

| the | ? | How's | today | weather |

····▶ _____

오늘 날씨가 어때?

2

| . | snowing | It's |

····▶ _____

눈이 와.

3

| there | How's | weather | ? | the |

····▶ _____

거기 날씨는 어때?

4

| hot | . | It's | and | sunny |

····▶ _____

날이 덥고 화창해.

5

| windy | ? | Is | it |

····▶ _____

바람이 부니?

Put on Your Coat

Words

A Look and check.

1

hat ⬜   sunglasses ⬜

2

boots ⬜   shorts ⬜

3

T-shirt ⬜   coat ⬜

4

hat ⬜   jacket ⬜

5

raincoat ⬜   boots ⬜

6

sunglasses ⬜   coat ⬜

7

jacket ⬜   T-shirt ⬜

8

shorts ⬜   raincoat ⬜

Practice

A Read and match.

1 Put on your jacket.

2 Put on your hat.

3 Put on your boots.

4 Put on your T-shirt.

B Write and circle.

| shorts | hat | coat | raincoat |

1 It's cold.

   Put on your _____.

2 It's raining.

   Put on your _____.

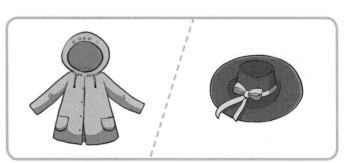

Listen & Talk

(A) Read and match.

1

> It's hot.
> Put on your shorts.

2

> It's raining.
> Put on your raincoat.

3

> It's snowing.
> Put on your boots.

4

> It's sunny.
> Put on your sunglasses.

(B) Look and write.

| Put on | raining | windy | raincoat |

1

A: It's _____.

Put on your _____.

B: Okay, Dad.

2

A: It's _____ today.

_____ your jacket.

B: Okay.

28

Write & Talk

A Look and write.

1

A: It's cold outside.

Put on your _____.

B: Okay, thank you.

2

A: How's the _____?

B: It's windy. Put on your _____.

A: Okay.

3

A: It's _____ today.

Put on your _____ and _____.

B: Okay, Mom.

4

A: It's _____.

Take your _____.

B: Okay.

5

A: How's the weather today?

B: It's _____.

Take your _____.

A: Okay.

Story

A Look and write.

| I like my raincoat. | Put on your sunglasses. | Put on your T-shirt. |

1
It's hot.
_____

Okay.

2
Oh, it's sunny.
_____

Okay.

B Look and write.

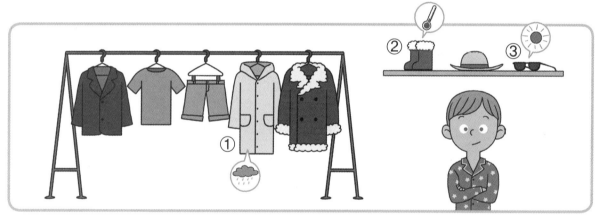

1 A: It's _____. Put on _____ _____.

   B: Okay.

2 A: It's _____. Put on your _____.

   B: Okay.

3 A: How's the weather?

   B: It's _____. _____ your _____.

   A: Okay.

Writing

A Make the sentence.

1

| on | . | your | Put | boots |

····▶ _____

네 부츠를 신어라.

2

| your | jacket | on | Put | . |

····▶ _____

네 재킷을 입어라.

3

| . | shorts | Put | your | on |

····▶ _____

네 반바지를 입어라.

4

| raining | . | It's | today |

····▶ _____

오늘 비가 와.

5

| your | Take | umbrella | . |

····▶ _____

네 우산을 가져가.

UNIT 3 She's My Friend

Words

Ⓐ Complete the puzzle.

1
f

2

3

3

4

5

7

6

→ Across   ↓ Down

3    1

4    2

5    3

6    7

strong

young

old

tall

mother

father

sister

brother

Practice

Ⓐ Circle and write.

1   She's my _____.
           (mother / sister)

2   He's my _____.
           (brother / father)

3   _____ my sister.
  (She's / He's)

4   _____ my brother.
  (She's / He's)

Ⓑ Follow and circle.

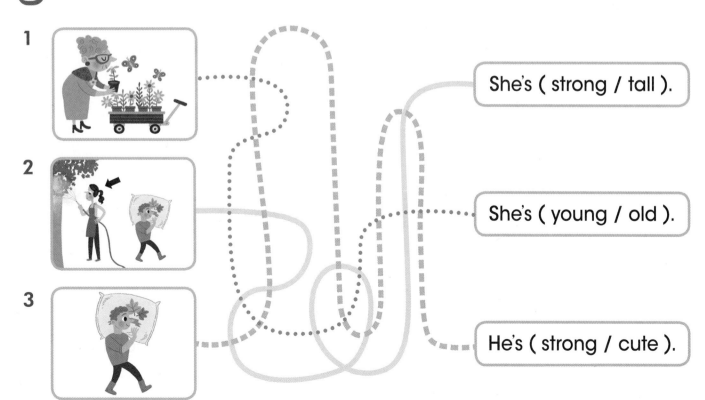

1

She's (strong / tall).

2

She's (young / old).

3

He's (strong / cute).

Listen & Talk

(A) Circle and write.

1

A: Who is _____?

B: He's my _____.
(father / grandfather)

2

A: Who is _____?

B: She's my _____.
(sister / brother)

3

A: He's _____. Who is _____?
(tall / strong)

B: He's my uncle.

(B) Look and write.

| tall | cute | she | he | Who |

1

A: Who is _____?

B: He's my brother.

He's _____.

2

A: _____ is _____?

B: She's my friend, Jenny.

She's _____.

Write & Talk

A Look and write.

1

A: Who is _____?

B: He's my _____.

2

A: _____ is she?

B: _____ my mother.

3

A: She's _____.

   Who is _____?

B: She's my friend, Lucia.

4

A: Who _____ _____?

B: He's my grandfather.

A: _____ cool.

5

A: Do you have a sister?

B: _____, I do. She's my _____, Kelly.

A: Oh, _____ cute.

Story

A Look and match.

1

ⓐ **A:** He's my dog, Max.
B: He's nice!

2

ⓑ **A:** She's strong. Who is she?
B: She's my mother.

3

ⓒ **A:** He's tall. Who is he?
B: He's my father.

B Look and write.

1

A: Look! _____ cool.

_____ is he?

B: _____ my brother.

2

A: Who is _____?

B: _____ my sister, Kate.

A: Oh, _____ very cute.

Writing

Ⓐ Make the sentence.

1

| is | ? | she | Who |

····▶ _____

그녀는 누구야?

2

| he | ? | Who | is |

····▶ _____

그는 누구야?

3

| mother | my | She's | . |

····▶ _____

그녀는 나의 어머니셔.

4

| young | . | He's |

····▶ _____

그는 어려.

5

| strong | He's | . | very |

····▶ _____

그는 매우 힘이 세.

Is He a Firefighter?

Words

A Trace and match.

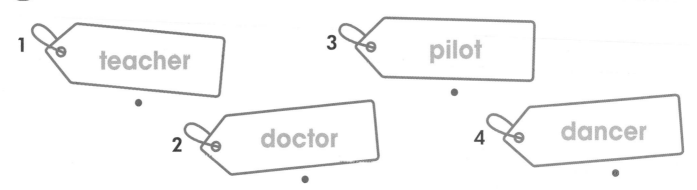

1   teacher

3   pilot

2   doctor

4   dancer

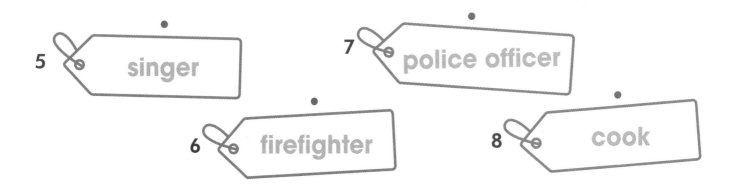

5   singer

7   police officer

6   firefighter

8   cook

Practice

A Read and mark O or X.

1

He's a doctor.

2

She's a police officer.

3

He's a pilot.

4

She's a teacher.

B Look and circle.

1

A: Is he a dancer?

B: (Yes, he is. / No, he isn't.)

2

A: Is she a singer?

B: (Yes, she is. / No, she isn't.)

3

A: Is he a cook?

B: (Yes, he is. / No, he isn't.)

Listen & Talk

A Read and check.

1

A: ☐ Is she a firefighter?
☐ Is she a police officer?

B: Yes, she is.

2

A: Is he a doctor?

B: ☐ Yes, he is.
☐ No, he isn't. He's a pilot.

3

A: Is she a teacher?

B: ☐ No, she isn't. She's a singer.
☐ No, she isn't. She's a cook.

B Look and write.

| teacher firefighter cool pretty |

1

A: Is she a _____?

B: Yes, _____ _____.

_____ pretty.

2

A: _____ _____ a pilot?

B: No, he isn't. He's a _____.

A: He's _____.

40

Write & Talk

A Look and write.

1

A: Is he a _____?

B: Yes, _____ _____.

2

A: Is _____ a teacher?

B: _____, she isn't. She's a _____.

3

A: _____ _____ a firefighter?

B: No, he isn't. He's a _____.

4

A: Look! She's pretty.

Is she a _____?

B: No, _____ isn't. She's a _____.

5

A: Is he your dad?

B: Yes, _____ _____.

A: _____ he a _____?

B: Yes, he is.

Story

(A) Look and write.

She's a pilot.	Is he a firefighter?	Is she a police officer?

1

_____

Yes, he is.

2

_____

No, she isn't.

_____

(B) Look and write.

1

A: Is she a _____?

B: Yes, _____ _____.

2

A: Is _____ a _____?

B: Yes, she is. _____ pretty.

3

A: Is _____ a doctor?

B: _____, he _____.

He's a _____.

42

Writing

Ⓐ Make the sentence.

1

| a | . | He's | cook |

···▶ _____

그는 요리사야.

2

| . | firefighter | a | She's |

···▶ _____

그녀는 소방관이야.

3

| she | ? | Is | singer | a |

···▶ _____

그녀는 가수니?

4

| ? | a | Is | pilot | he |

···▶ _____

그는 파일럿이니?

5

| he | ? | teacher | Is | a |

···▶ _____

그는 선생님이니?

How Old Is She?

Words

(A) Check and write.

1
- ☐ seventeen
- ☐ fourteen

_____

2
- ☐ nineteen
- ☐ thirteen

_____

3
- ☐ fifteen
- ☐ sixteen

_____

4
- ☐ eleven
- ☐ twelve

_____

5
- ☐ nineteen
- ☐ eleven

_____

6
- ☐ thirteen
- ☐ twelve

_____

7
- ☐ sixteen
- ☐ eighteen

_____

8
- ☐ fifteen
- ☐ seventeen

_____

9
- ☐ fourteen
- ☐ nineteen

_____

Practice

A Read and mark O or X.

1 I'm eighteen years old.

2 I'm nineteen years old.

3 I'm sixteen.

4 I'm eleven.

B Circle and write.

1 A: How old is _____?
          (she / he)

B: She's _____ years old.
     (twelve / thirteen)

2 A: How old is _____?
          (she / he)

B: He's _____ years old.
     (fourteen / fifteen)

Listen & Talk

(A) Circle and match.

1  How old is [he / she] ? •   • She's twelve.

2  How old is [he / she] ? •   • She's fifteen.

3  How old is [he / she] ? •   • He's nineteen.

(B) Look and write.

| eleven | thirteen | She's | she | How old |

1

A: _____ is he?

B: He's _____ years old.

2

A: _____ my sister, Jane.

B: How old is _____?

A: She's _____.

Write & Talk

Ⓐ Look and write.

1

A: How _____ are you?

B: I'm _____ years old.

2

A: She's great!

How old _____ _____?

B: She's _____.

3

A: He's Mike.

B: How old _____ _____?

A: He's _____.

4

A: Is he your brother?

B: _____, he is.

A: How old is _____?

B: He's _____.

5

A: What's your _____?

B: I'm Julia.

A: _____ _____ are you?

B: _____ ten.

Story

A Match and write.

1

A: How _____ is _____?

B: He's _____.

2

A: How old is _____?

B: She's _____.

3

A: _____ are you?

B: _____ ten.

B Look and write.

1 A: How old _____ _____?

   B: He's _____.

2 A: _____ _____ is she?

   B: She's _____ years old.

3 A: Is _____ your brother?

   B: _____, he is.

   A: How old _____ _____?

   B: He's _____.

Writing

(A) Make the sentence.

1

| old | ? | is | she | How |

...▸ _____

그녀는 몇 살이에요?

2

| years | . | She's | old | thirteen |

...▸ _____

그녀는 13살이야.

3

| years | eleven | He's | . | old |

...▸ _____

그는 11살이에요.

4

| ? | old | you | are | How |

...▸ _____

너는 몇 살이니?

5

| . | old | I'm | fifteen | years |

...▸ _____

나는 15살이야.

UNIT 6 What Day Is It Today?

Words

A Trace, find, and match.

1

Sunday
•

2

Fri.

Friday
•

3

Tuesday
•

4

Monday
•

STUESDAYTPKFRIDAYTUYSUNDAYTWTIMONDAYKQ

WTHURSDAYKCPUKIWEDNESDAYDISATURDAYSCK

•   •   •

5

Saturday

6

Thursday

7

Wednesday

Practice

A Look and check.

1
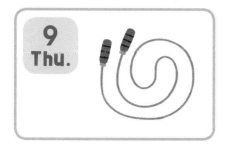

☐ It's Thursday.
☐ It's Tuesday.

2

☐ It's Friday.
☐ It's Monday.

3

☐ It's Wednesday.
☐ It's Saturday.

4

☐ It's Sunday.
☐ It's Tuesday.

B Look and write.

| Wednesday | Friday | What | day |

1

A: What _____ is it today?

B: It's _____ .

2

A: _____ day is it today?

B: It's _____ .

Listen & Talk

A Match and write.

1 Saturday

2 Sunday

3 Tuesday

It's _____.
We have pizza today.

It's _____.
We have onion soup today.

It's _____.
We have chicken today.

B Look and write.

onion soup   carrot pie   Monday   Thursday

1

THU

A: What _____ is it today?

B: It's _____.

We have _____ today.

2

MON

A: What day _____ _____ today?

B: It's _____.

We have _____ today.

Write & Talk

A Look and write.

1

A: _____ day is _____ today?

B: It's ____ _____.

2

A: What _____ is it today?

B: It's _____.

We can cook today.

3

A: _____ day is it _____?

B: It's _____.

We _____ bread and milk.

4

A: Today is _____.

We have _____ soup.

B: I _____ like mushroom soup.

5

A: What day _____ _____ today?

B: It's _____. It's my birthday.

A: Happy birthday, Kate!

Story

A Match and write.

1

    I can _____ today.

2

    A: What _____ is it today?

    B: It's _____.

3

    A: _____ day is it today?

    B: _____ Thursday.

B Look and write.

1

A: _____ _____ is it today?

B: It's _____.

A: Oh, we can ski today.

2

A: What day is _____ _____?

B: It's _____. We have fish today.

A: Oh, I like fish.

Writing

Ⓐ Make the sentence.

1

| day | ? | is | What | today | it |

····▶ _____

오늘은 무슨 요일이니?

2

| . | Wednesday | today | It's |

····▶ _____

오늘은 수요일이야.

3

| Tuesday | . | It's | today |

····▶ _____

오늘은 화요일이야.

4

| can | . | We | today | ski |

····▶ _____

우리는 오늘 스키 탈 수 있어.

5

| pizza | today | have | . | We |

····▶ _____

우리는 오늘 피자를 먹어.

UNIT 7 It Has Big Wings

Words

A Look and write.

1

_____

2

_____

3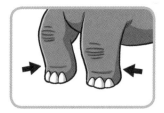

_____

4

_____

5

_____

eyes

a nose

feet

a mouth

ears

a tail

a neck

wings

legs

6

_____

7

_____

8

_____

9

_____

Practice

A Look and match.

1

- It has big ears.
- It has long legs.
- It has big feet.
- It has a long neck.

2

B Circle and write.

1

A: Look at the _____. (giraffe / bird)

B: It has _____ wings. (big / small)

2

A: Look at the _____. (hippo / elephant)

B: It has a _____ tail. (long / short)

Listen & Talk

A Read and match.

1 Look at the rabbit. •

2 Look at the owl. •

3 Look at the pig. •

• It has big eyes.

• It has long ears.

• It has short legs.

B Look and write.

monkey   bear   long   big   tail   feet

1

A: Look at the _____ .

B: It has _____ _____ .

2

A: Look! Is it a _____ ?

B: Yes, it is. It has a _____ _____ .

58

Write & Talk

Ⓐ Look and write.

1

A: Look at the _____.

B: It has _____ legs.

2

A: _____ at the bird.

B: It _____ big _____.

3

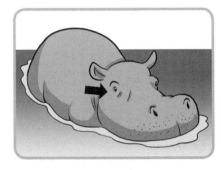

A: Look! _____ _____ a hippo?

B: Yes, it is. It has _____ _____.

4

A: Look! Is it a fox?

B: _____, it is.

It _____ big _____.

5

A: Look _____ the shark.

B: _____ big.

A: It _____ a big _____.

Story

A Look and write the letter.

1

a Yes, that's right.

c Is it a koala?

2

b It has a big nose.
It's gray. What is it?

B Look and write.

1 A: Look at the _____.

B: It has small _____.

2 A: Look at the _____.

B: It _____ long _____.

3 A: Is it a panda?

B: _____, it is.

_____ has a short _____.

4 A: _____ _____ an owl?

B: Yes, it is.

It has _____ _____.

Writing

A Make the sentence.

1

at Look bird the .

····▶ _____

새 좀 봐.

2

monkey Look . the at

····▶ _____

원숭이 좀 봐.

3

has ears It . big

····▶ _____

그것은 큰 귀를 가지고 있어.

4

short . It legs has

····▶ _____

그것은 짧은 다리를 가지고 있어.

5

big It . mouth has a

····▶ _____

그것은 큰 입을 가지고 있어.

I'm in the Bathroom

Words

Ⓐ **Look and write.**

bathroom	dining room	kitchen
living room	yard	bedroom

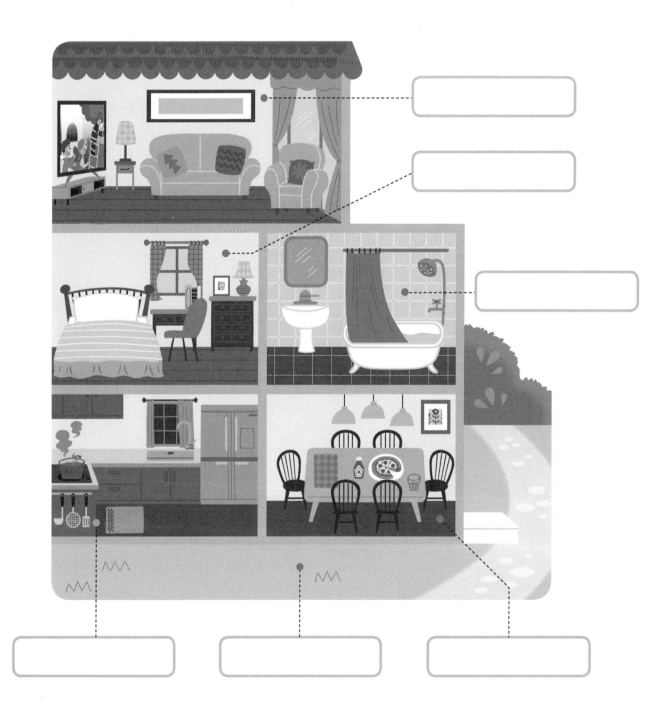

Practice

A Read and mark O or X.

1 He's in the kitchen.

2 She's in the bedroom.

3 She's in the living room.

4 He's in the yard.

B Circle and write.

1

A: Where is _____? (he / she)

B: He's in the _____.
(living room / dining room)

2

A: Where is _____? (he / she)

B: She's in the _____.
(bathroom / bedroom)

Listen & Talk

Ⓐ Read and match.

1 Where is Grandma? • • She's in the yard.

2 Where is Dad? • • He's in the bedroom.

3 Where are you, Lisa?  • • He's in the kitchen.

4 Where is Jack? • • I'm in the bathroom.

Ⓑ Circle and write.

| bathroom | living room | dining room | kitchen |

1

A: _____ is Julia?

B: (She's / He's) in the _____.

2

A: Where _____ you, John?

B: (He's / I'm) in the _____.

Write & Talk

Ⓐ Look and write.

1

A: Where are _____, Nick?

B: I'm _____ the _____.

2

A: _____ is Dad?

B: _____ in the _____.

3

A: Mom, I'm home.

_____ are you?

B: _____ in the _____.

4

A: Where _____ Tony?

B: _____ in the _____.

5

A: Where are you, Mike?

B: I'm here. _____ in the _____.

A: _____ is Lisa?

B: She's _____ the living room.

Story

(A) Look and write.

| She's in the bedroom. | I'm in the living room. | Where is Kate? |

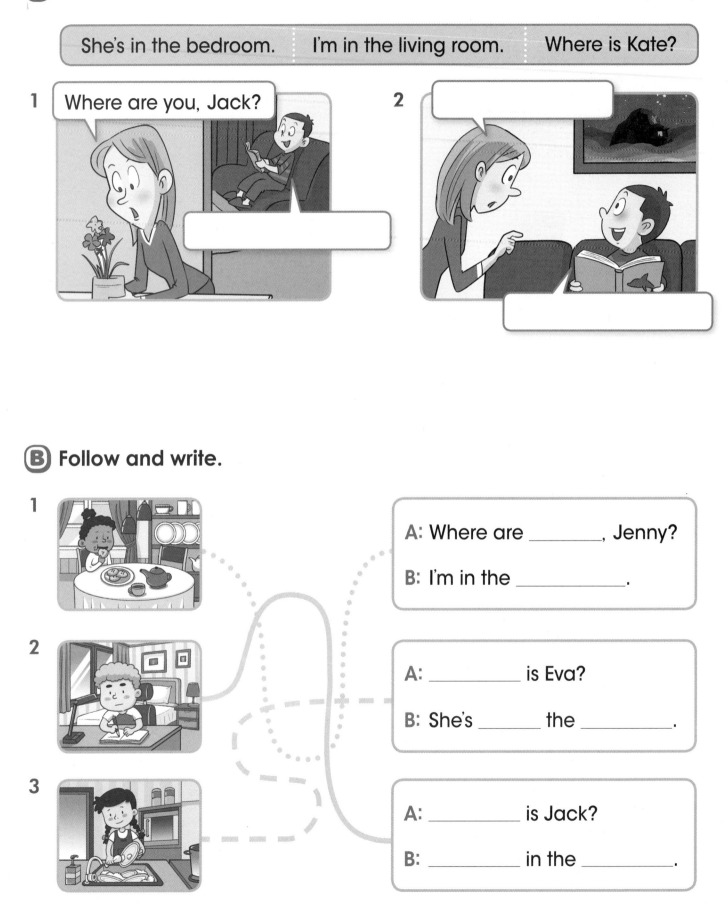

1 Where are you, Jack?

2

(B) Follow and write.

1
A: Where are _____, Jenny?

B: I'm in the _____.

2
A: _____ is Eva?

B: She's _____ the _____.

3
A: _____ is Jack?

B: _____ in the _____.

Writing

Ⓐ Make the sentence.

1

| Lucy | ? | is | Where |

·····▶ _____

루시는 어디에 있어요?

2

| ? | are | Where | you |

·····▶ _____

너는 어디에 있니?

3

| . | in | living room | I'm | the |

·····▶ _____

나는 거실에 있어.

4

| kitchen | He's | the | . | in |

·····▶ _____

그는 부엌에 계셔.

5

| in | . | dining room | the | She's |

·····▶ _____

그녀는 식당에 있어.